U.S.A. TRAVEL GUIDES

MISSISSIPPI

BY ANN HEINRICHS • ILLUSTRATED BY MATT KANIA

JAN 2021

The Child's World®
childsworld.com

Published by The Child's World®
1980 Lookout Drive • Mankato, MN 56003-1705
800-599-READ • www.childsworld.com

ISBN 9781503819641
LCCN 2016961177

Printing
Printed in the United States of America
PA02334

Ann Heinrichs is the author of more than 100 books for children and young adults. She has also enjoyed successful careers as a children's book editor and an advertising copywriter. Ann grew up in Fort Smith, Arkansas, and lives in Chicago, Illinois.

About the Author
Ann Heinrichs

Matt Kania loves maps and, as a kid, dreamed of making them. In school he studied geography and cartography, and today he makes maps for a living. Matt's favorite thing about drawing maps is learning about the places they represent. Many of the maps he has created can be found in books, magazines, videos, Web sites, and public places.

About the
Map Illustrator
Matt Kania

On the cover: State lawmakers work inside the capitol in Jackson.

OUR MISSISSIPPI TRIP

MISSISSIPPI

Are you ready to explore Mississippi? You'll be glad you came. There's so much to discover here!

You'll see shrimp boats and alligators. You'll meet blues singers and visit Elvis Presley's birthplace. You'll make inventions and watch hot-air balloons race across the sky. And you'll eat slugburgers and sweet potato pie!

See how much there is to do? Let's not wait another minute. Just buckle up that seat belt. We're on our way!

WELCOME TO
MISSISSIPPI

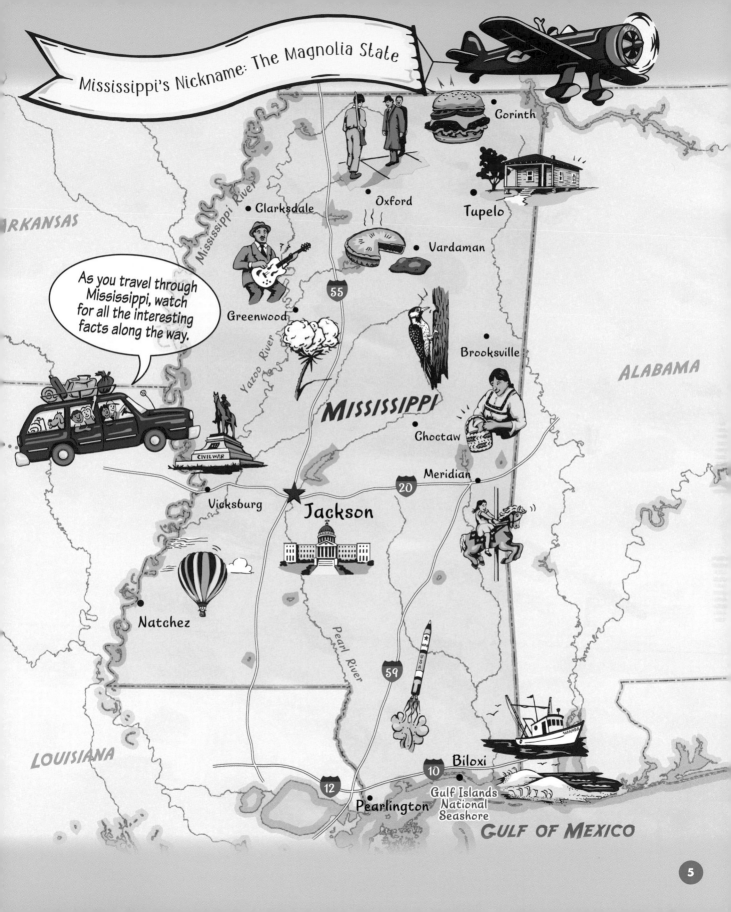

Mississippi's Nickname: The Magnolia State

As you travel through Mississippi, watch for all the interesting facts along the way.

ARKANSAS

Mississippi River

Clarksdale

Oxford

Corinth

Tupelo

Vardaman

Greenwood

55

Yazoo River

MISSISSIPPI

Brooksville

ALABAMA

Choctaw

Meridian

20

Vicksburg

Jackson

Natchez

Pearl River

59

Biloxi

10

Gulf Islands National Seashore

LOUISIANA

12

Pearlington

GULF OF MEXICO

CIVIL WAR

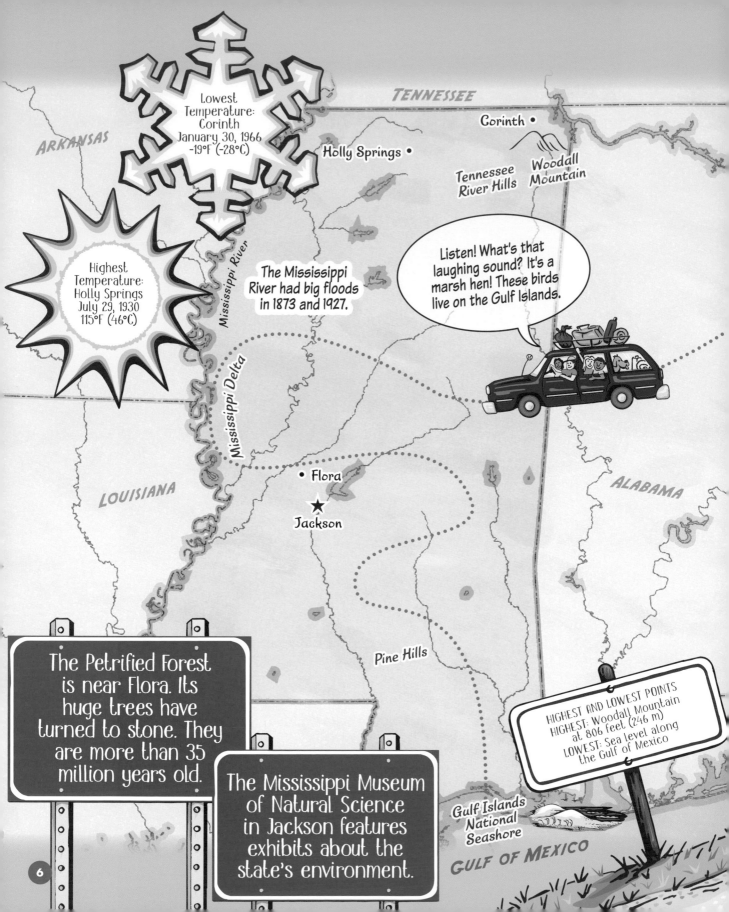

Lowest Temperature:
Corinth
January 30, 1966
-19°F (-28°C)

Highest Temperature:
Holly Springs
July 29, 1930
115°F (46°C)

TENNESSEE

Corinth •

Holly Springs •

Tennessee River Hills

Woodall Mountain

ARKANSAS

The Mississippi River had big floods in 1873 and 1927.

Listen! What's that laughing sound? It's a marsh hen! These birds live on the Gulf Islands.

Mississippi River

Mississippi Delta

LOUISIANA

• Flora

★ Jackson

ALABAMA

Pine Hills

The Petrified Forest is near Flora. Its huge trees have turned to stone. They are more than 35 million years old.

The Mississippi Museum of Natural Science in Jackson features exhibits about the state's environment.

HIGHEST AND LOWEST POINTS
HIGHEST: Woodall Mountain at 806 feet (246 m)
LOWEST: Sea level along the Gulf of Mexico

Gulf Islands National Seashore

GULF OF MEXICO

Wiggle your toes in the white sand. Watch a sunset over the water. Ride a bike for miles along the shore. Or jump right in for a swim. You're on Gulf Islands National Seashore! These islands lie off Mississippi's coast. Southern Mississippi faces the Gulf of Mexico.

The Mississippi River is the state's major river. It runs along the whole western border. Land along the river is very fertile. This region is called the Mississippi Delta. Rolling hills cover much of Mississippi. The Tennessee River Hills are in the northeast. In the southeast are the Pine Hills. They're sometimes called the Piney Woods.

Relax on the white sand beaches on Mississippi's coast.

Bullfrogs are croaking. Wild turkeys are gobbling. Squirrels are barking. Red-cockaded woodpeckers are rapping and tapping. You're exploring the Sam D. Hamilton Noxubee National Wildlife Refuge near Brooksville. It can be pretty noisy!

Lots of animals make their homes in Mississippi. Some live in forests. Others live in wetlands.

White-tailed deer live in much of the state. They have their **fawns** in early summer. Squirrels, rabbits, and raccoons are common, too.

You'll see alligators in wetland areas. Sometimes they swim or rest in the water. Their eyes stick out above the water. Then they can see what's going on!

Watch out for alligators in the Sam D. Hamilton Noxubee National Wildlife Refuge.

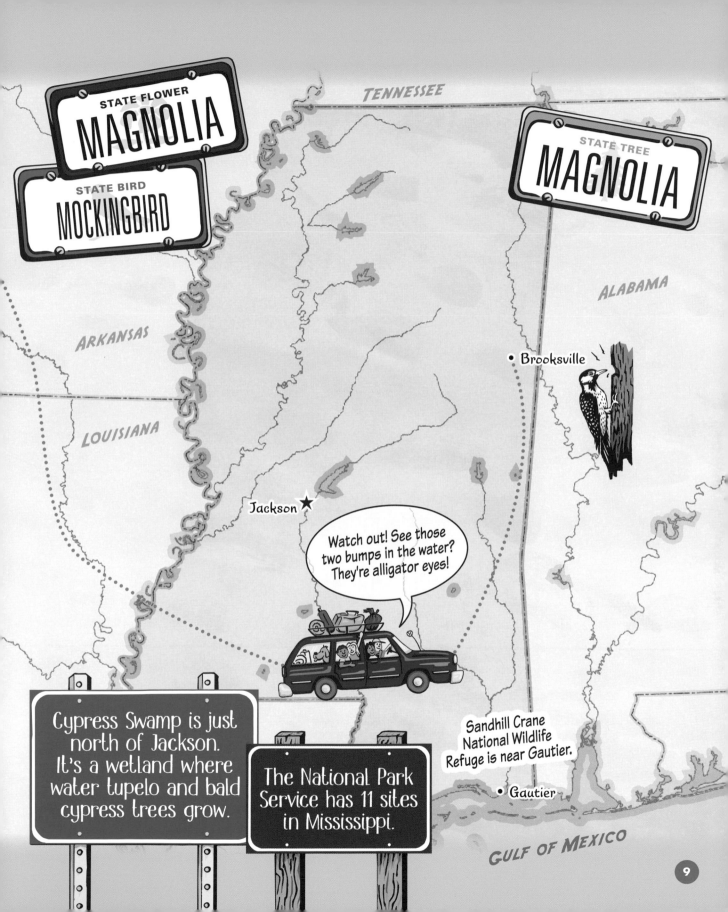

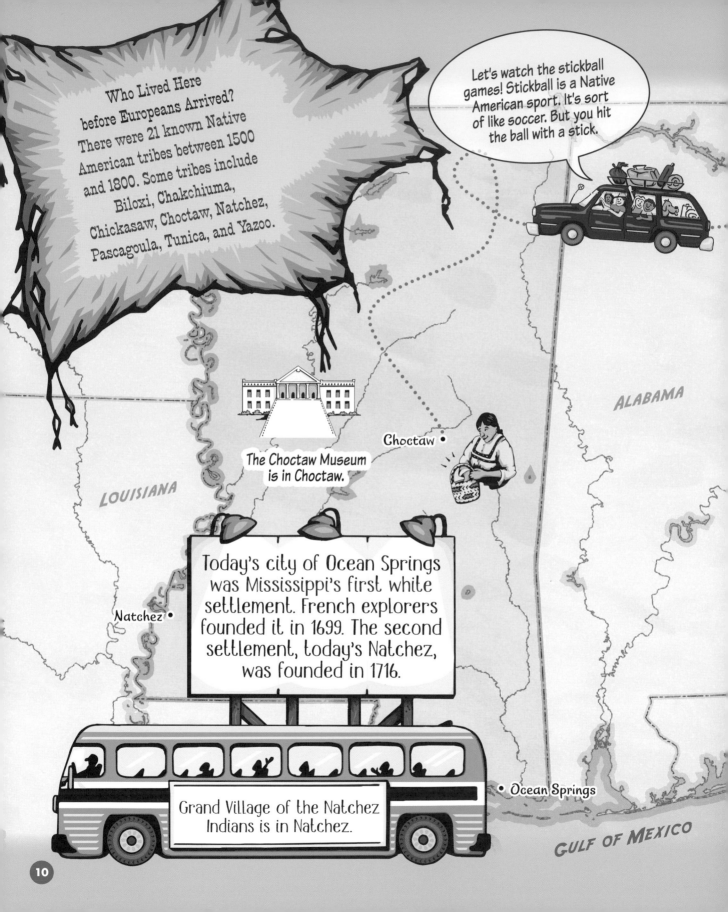

Who Lived Here before Europeans Arrived? There were 21 known Native American tribes between 1500 and 1800. Some tribes include Biloxi, Chakchiuma, Chickasaw, Choctaw, Natchez, Pascagoula, Tunica, and Yazoo.

Let's watch the stickball games! Stickball is a Native American sport. It's sort of like soccer. But you hit the ball with a stick.

ALABAMA

Choctaw •

The Choctaw Museum is in Choctaw.

LOUISIANA

Today's city of Ocean Springs was Mississippi's first white settlement. French explorers founded it in 1699. The second settlement, today's Natchez, was founded in 1716.

Natchez •

• Ocean Springs

Grand Village of the Natchez Indians is in Natchez.

GULF OF MEXICO

THE CHOCTAW INDIAN FAIR IN CHOCTAW

Watch the dancers tell stories with their moves. Colorful feathers, beads, and fringe decorate their costumes. Then try some delicious **hominy** or **fry bread**. It's the Choctaw Indian Fair!

The fair takes place in July every year. It has historical and cultural exhibits, arts and crafts, Choctaw stickball, carnival rides, and games.

Thousands of Native Americans live in Mississippi. Their ancestors hunted in the forests and grew crops. They explain their history with many **legends**.

Today, the Mississippi Band of Choctaw Indians has 10,000 members. The tribe has more than 35,000 acres of land.

There are many handmade items found at the Choctaw Indian Fair.

STANTON HALL PLANTATION

When you visit Stanton Hall **Plantation** in Natchez, it's almost like stepping back in time! This beautiful home was built in 1859. Today, visitors can receive daily tours and view large rooms filled with antique furniture.

Mississippi has many plantations for visitors to explore. The land surrounding these historic homes was used to grow crops. Dozens of enslaved African American people were forced to work the fields.

Cotton was one crop that slaves harvested. Plantation owners had huge cotton farms. Slaves worked long hours on the farms without pay. They lived in small cabins. The plantation owners' homes were beautiful **mansions**.

Natchez has more than 10 historic buildings for visitors to see.

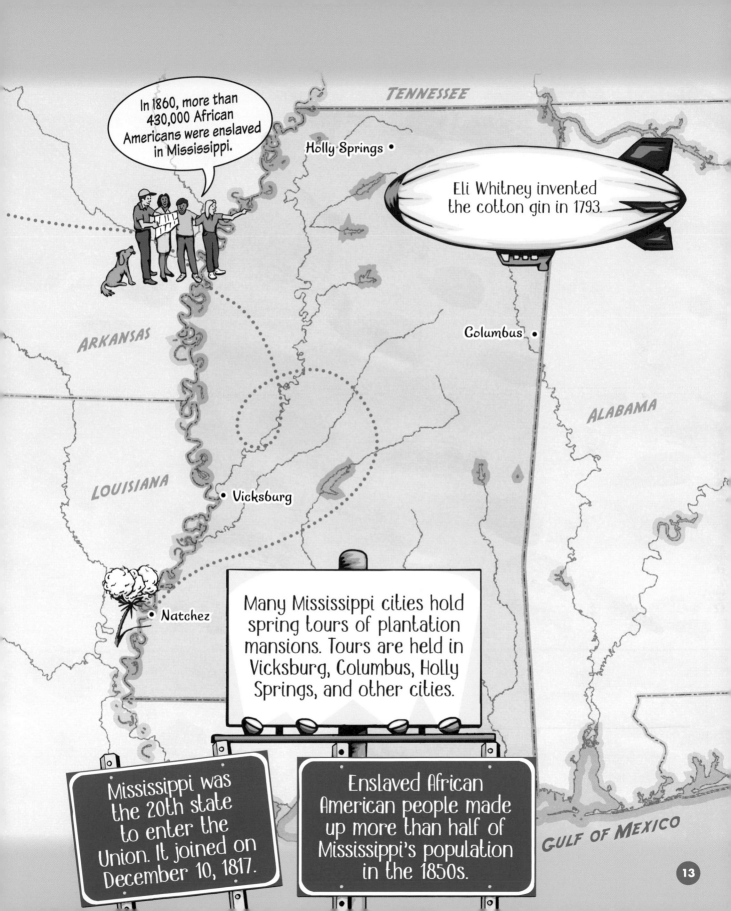

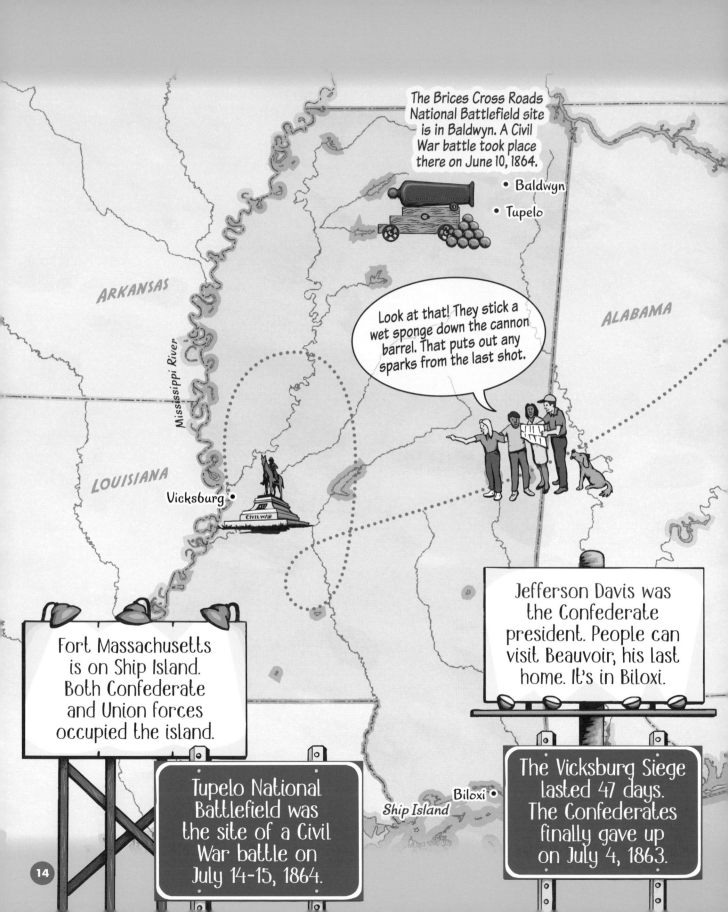

VICKSBURG NATIONAL MILITARY PARK

How do you fire an 1800s cannon? Just visit Vicksburg National Military Park. Cannon demonstrations there teach you how it's done.

This site was a battlefield in the Civil War (1861–1865). Northern and Southern states fought this war. The two sides disagreed about slavery. The North opposed slavery. But Southern plantations depended on the enslaved peoples' labor. Mississippi and other Southern states left the Union. They formed the Confederate States of America, or Confederacy.

The Union side won the Battle of Vicksburg. After that, the Union controlled the Mississippi River. The Union won the war, too.

Vicksburg National Military Park has cannon demonstrations for visitors to watch.

Are you sad sometimes? Then you could have the blues. It might help to sing some blues songs. They tell about being sad or lonely.

Blues songs began among African American people. One blues style is called Delta blues. It developed in the Mississippi Delta region. Just visit the Delta Blues Museum in Clarksdale. You'll learn all about early blues singers.

African Americans had good reasons to sing the blues. After the Civil War, enslaved people were freed. But many had nowhere to go. They stayed and worked as **sharecroppers**. This work kept them poor. They told about their feelings in blues songs.

It took many years after slavery ended before African Americans were given equal rights under the law.

Delta blues music started in Mississippi.

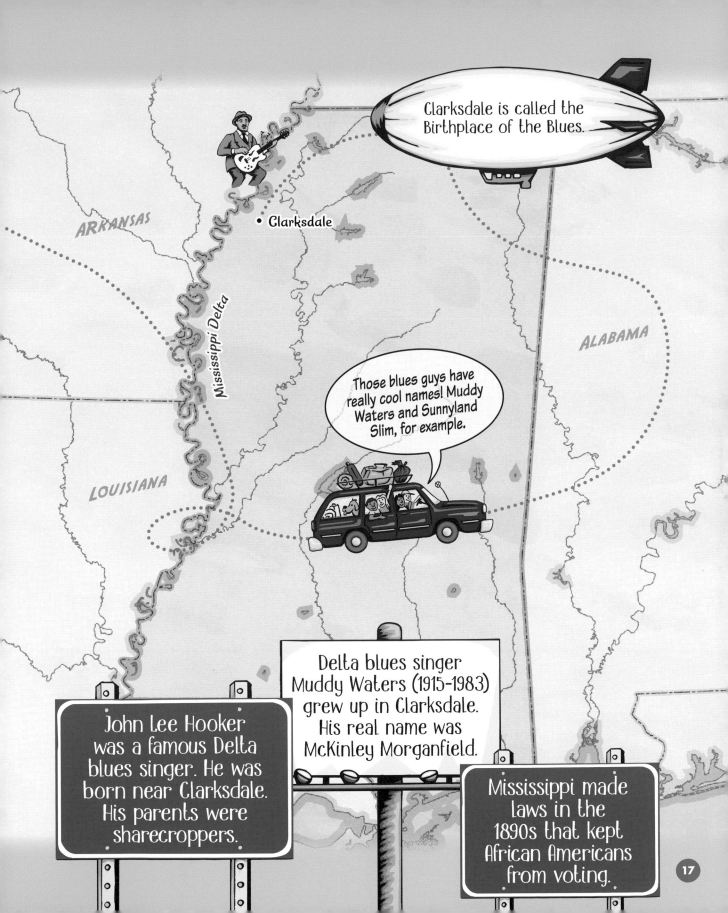

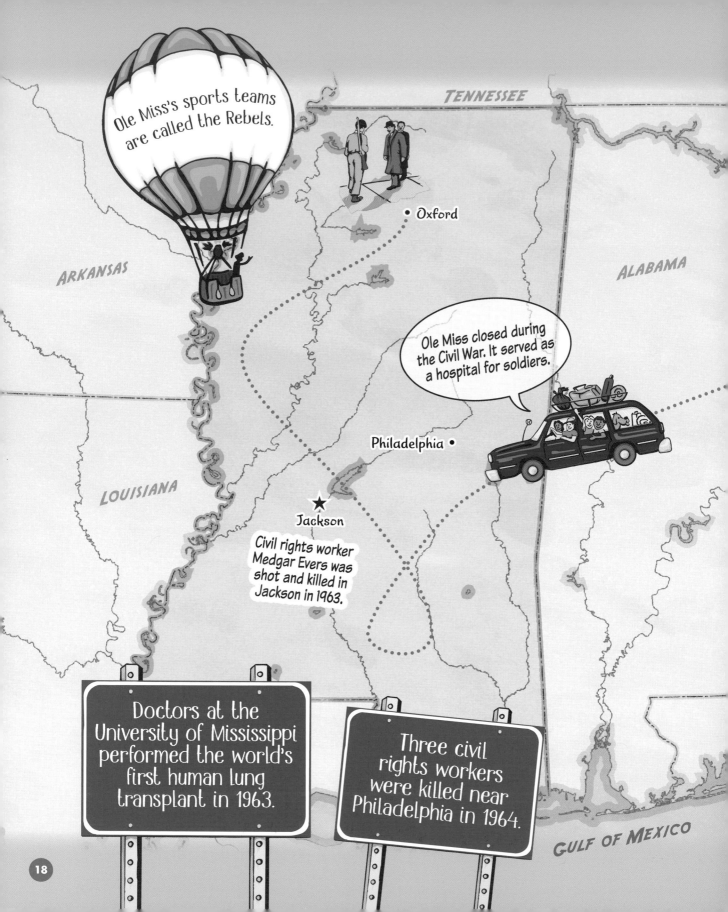

OLE MISS IN OXFORD

The University of Mississippi in Oxford opened in 1848. Its nickname is Ole Miss. Ole Miss was in the news in the 1960s. At that time, Mississippi schools were segregated. That is, African American and white students were separated. They could not attend the same schools.

In 1962, James Meredith was accepted for admission to Ole Miss. He would be its first African American student. Crowds of people protested, and **riots** broke out. President John F. Kennedy sent National Guard troops to Mississippi to keep order. At last, Meredith could safely begin his classes. There were many other **civil rights** struggles in Mississippi. It wasn't until 1970 that Mississippi schools were open to all students.

A monument at Old Miss is dedicated to James Meredith.

INFINITY SCIENCE CENTER

Take a look at the massive rocket engine. Then design and build your own invention. Or learn about hurricanes and the surface of planets. You're visiting the Infinity Science Center in Pearlington!

The Infinity Science Center teaches visitors about science, technology, engineering, and math. Visitors can watch live presentations, take bus tours, and jump on simulator rides!

The nation's space program sped up in the 1960s. Before that, Mississippi factories were busy during World War II (1939–1945). They made war supplies and built ships. Many military bases opened in Mississippi, too.

Learn about science, space, and more at the Infinity Science Center!

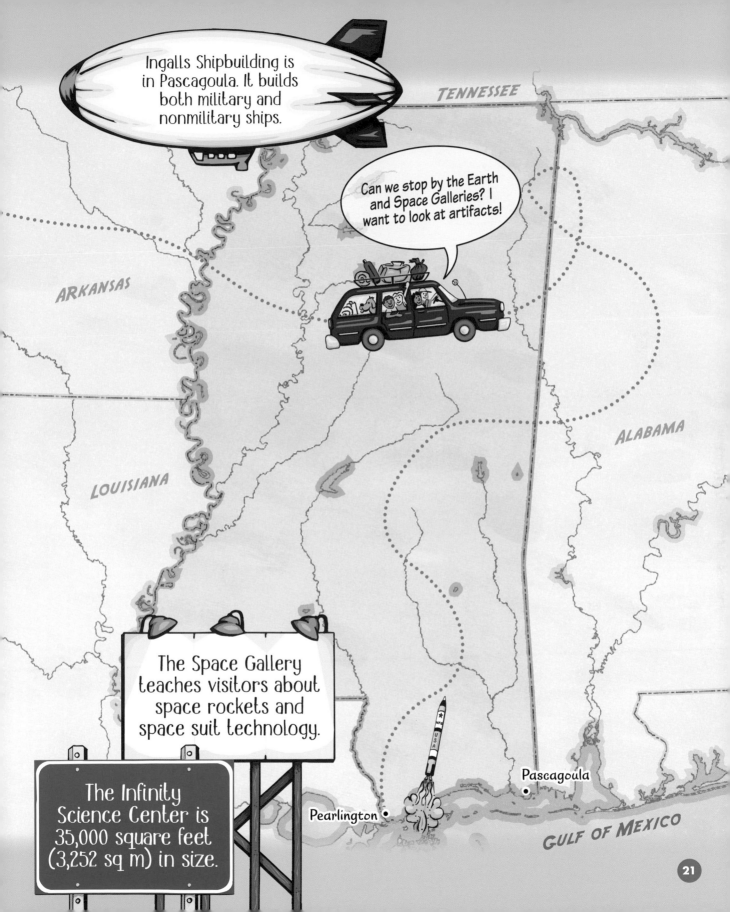

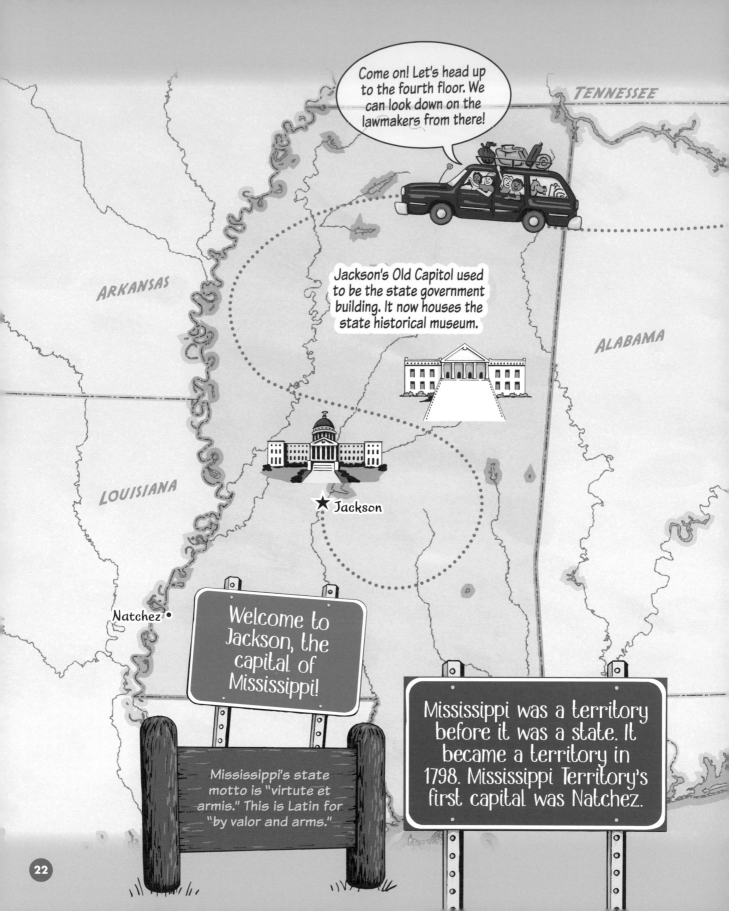

THE STATE CAPITOL IN JACKSON

Want to see government in action? Just visit the state capitol in Jackson. That's where Mississippi's state lawmakers work. You can watch them when they're meeting. They talk about laws they want to pass.

Mississippi's state government has three branches. The lawmakers make up one branch. They make the state laws. The governor heads another branch. This branch makes sure laws are carried out. Judges make up the third branch. They study the laws. Then they decide if laws have been broken.

Lawmakers meet in the capitol building in Jackson.

VARDAMAN'S SWEET POTATO FESTIVAL

Have you ever had sweet potato pie? It's delicious! There are lots of people who love it. They head for Vardaman's Sweet Potato Festival. Why? To enter the sweet potato pie-eating contest!

This festival celebrates a yummy Mississippi crop. Chickens are the state's top farm product. Cotton and soybeans are important field crops.

Forest trees are not exactly crops. But lumber from trees is very valuable. Mississippi has thousands of tree farms.

Catfish don't seem like farm animals, do they? But Mississippi's fish farmers raise tons of catfish. Most catfish farms are in the Mississippi Delta region.

Sweet potatoes are a tasty Mississippi crop!

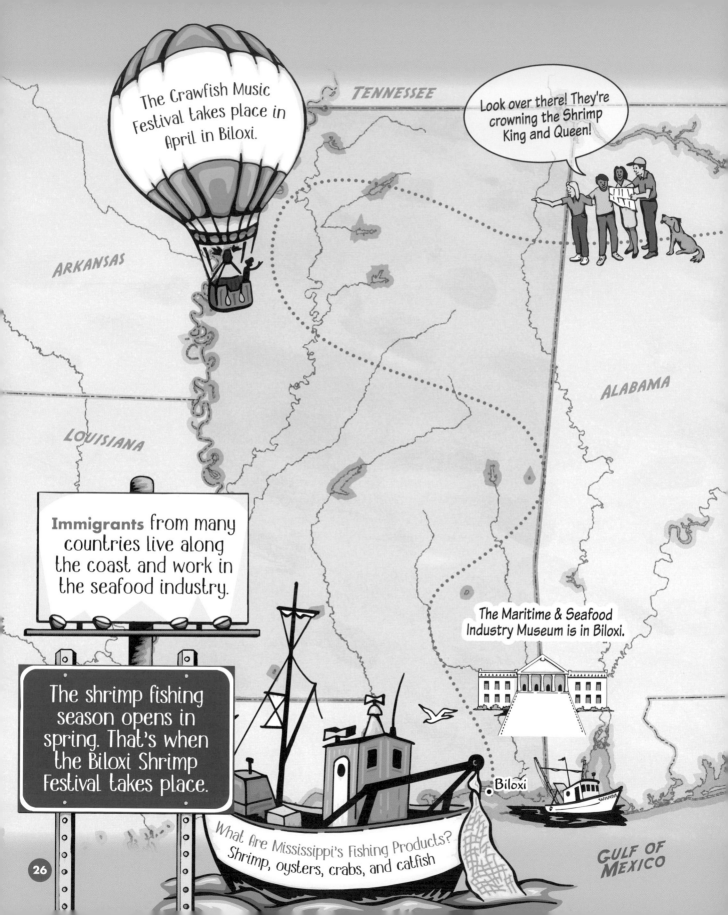

THE BLESSING OF THE FLEET

Shrimp fishing is a big **industry** in Mississippi. Shrimp fishers work long and hard. They spend hours out in their boats. There are always dangers, too. Storms can blow in quickly. Boats could turn over or spring a leak.

Because of these dangers, Biloxi holds a special event. It takes place in September at the Biloxi Shrimp Festival. First, a **wreath** is thrown into the water. This honors people lost at sea. Then colorfully decorated shrimp boats line up. A priest blesses them, one by one. This ceremony is the Blessing of the Fleet. Hundreds of people come to see it.

Shrimp fishing is no easy task. Workers have to haul shrimp onto their boats and sort through them.

THE SLUGBURGER FESTIVAL IN CORINTH

Come on by the SlugBurger Festival in Corinth. You'll love those juicy slugburgers!

Slugs are like snails with no shells. But don't worry. There are no slugs in slugburgers! They're made of beef and soybean meal.

Mississippians are good at making foods. In fact, foods are their major factory products. Many food plants package beef and chicken. Others make spices, drinks, and baked goods.

Mississippi makes lots of wood products, too. The wood comes from the state's forestlands. Pine is the most valuable wood. It's made into furniture and other wood products.

Today, Mississippi has more manufacturing jobs than jobs in agriculture.

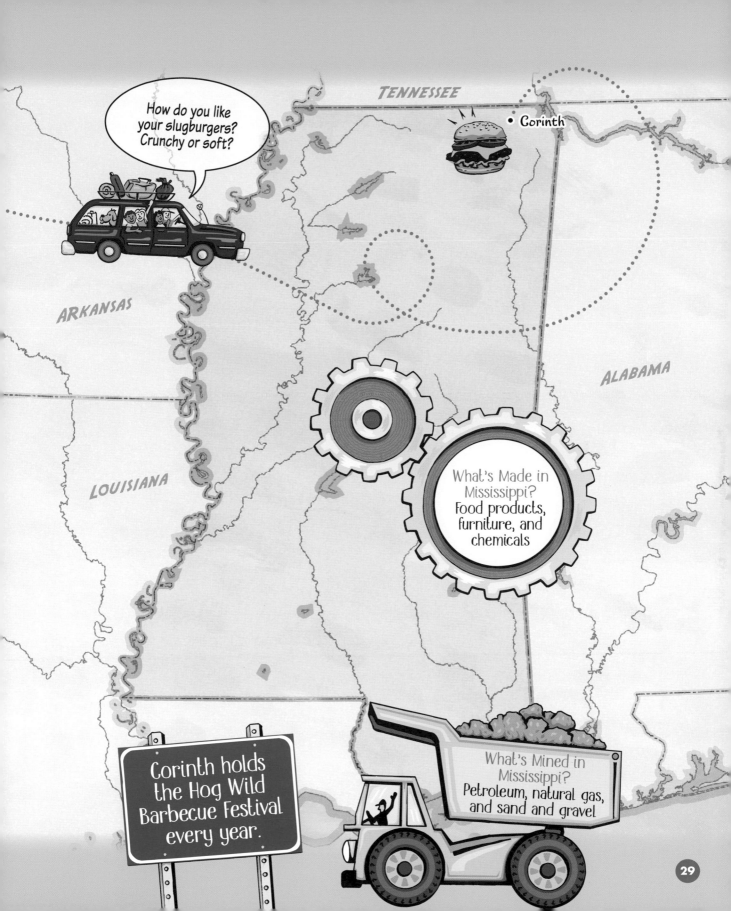

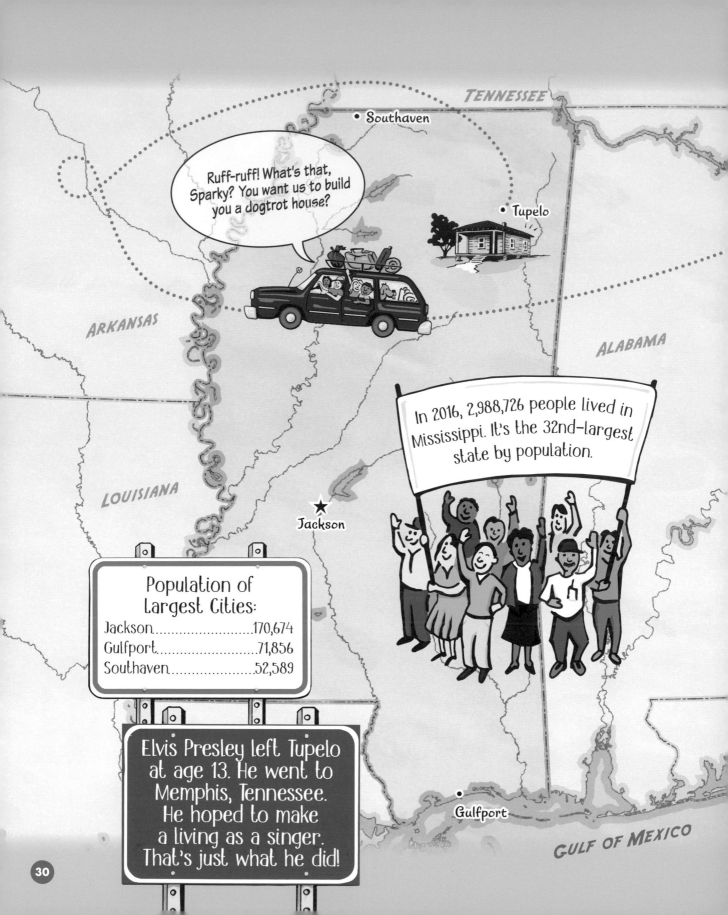

TENNESSEE

• Southhaven

Ruff-ruff! What's that, Sparky? You want us to build you a dogtrot house?

• Tupelo

ARKANSAS

ALABAMA

In 2016, 2,988,726 people lived in Mississippi. It's the 32nd-largest state by population.

LOUISIANA

★ Jackson

Population of Largest Cities:

Jackson.........................170,674
Gulfport..........................71,856
Southhaven.....................52,589

Elvis Presley left Tupelo at age 13. He went to Memphis, Tennessee. He hoped to make a living as a singer. That's just what he did!

• Gulfport

GULF OF MEXICO

ELVIS PRESLEY'S BIRTHPLACE

Have you heard of Elvis Presley? He was called the King of Rock and Roll.

Presley's birthplace is in Tupelo. The house where he was born has a door on each end. It's called a shotgun house. That's because someone could shoot straight through it. They'd shoot in one door and out the other!

Another old-time house was the dogtrot house. It had two big rooms. An open-air hall connected them. Outdoor dogs could trot through that hall!

These house styles were common in rural areas. Those are areas outside of cities and towns. Even today, much of Mississippi is rural. About half the people live in rural areas.

Elvis Presley was born in Tupelo. Visitors can still see the house where he was born.

THE GREAT MISSISSIPPI RIVER BALLOON RACE

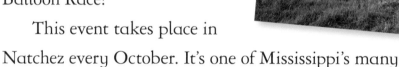

Hot-air balloons drift through the sky. Many of them have big, colorful stripes. They seem to be moving slowly. But they're racing. It's the Great Mississippi River Balloon Race!

This event takes place in Natchez every October. It's one of Mississippi's many colorful festivals. Some cities celebrate Mardi Gras. It's a carnival with parades and wild costumes.

There's always something fun to do in Mississippi. Many people go to the coast for vacation. Some like to tour plantations and mansions. Others visit museums and historic sites. Nature lovers go wandering through the woods. They enjoy peace and quiet for a change!

Colorful balloons fill the sky above Natchez every year.

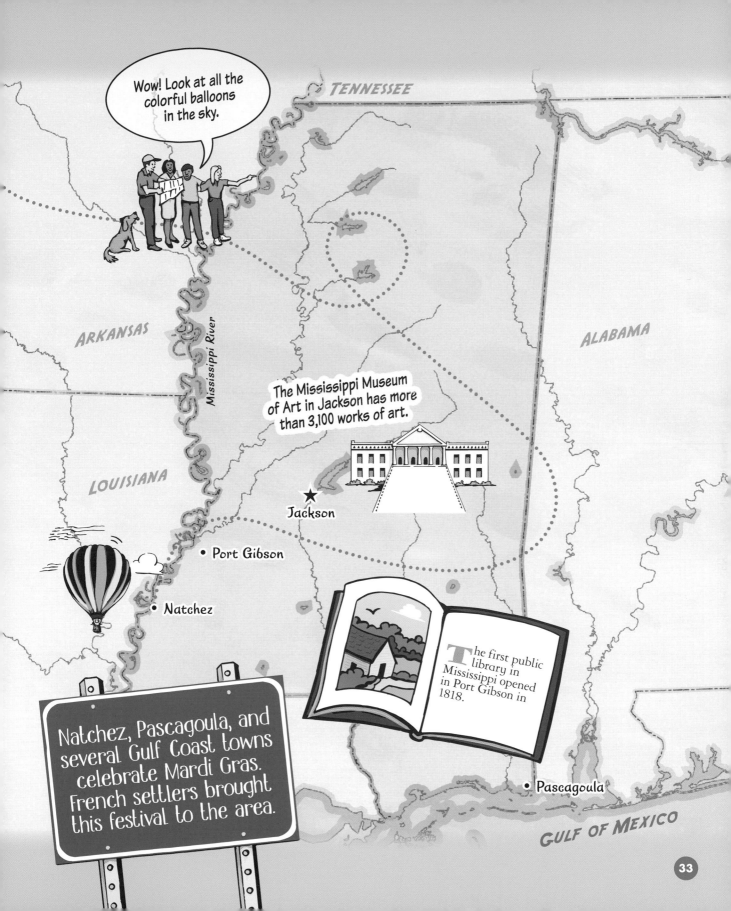

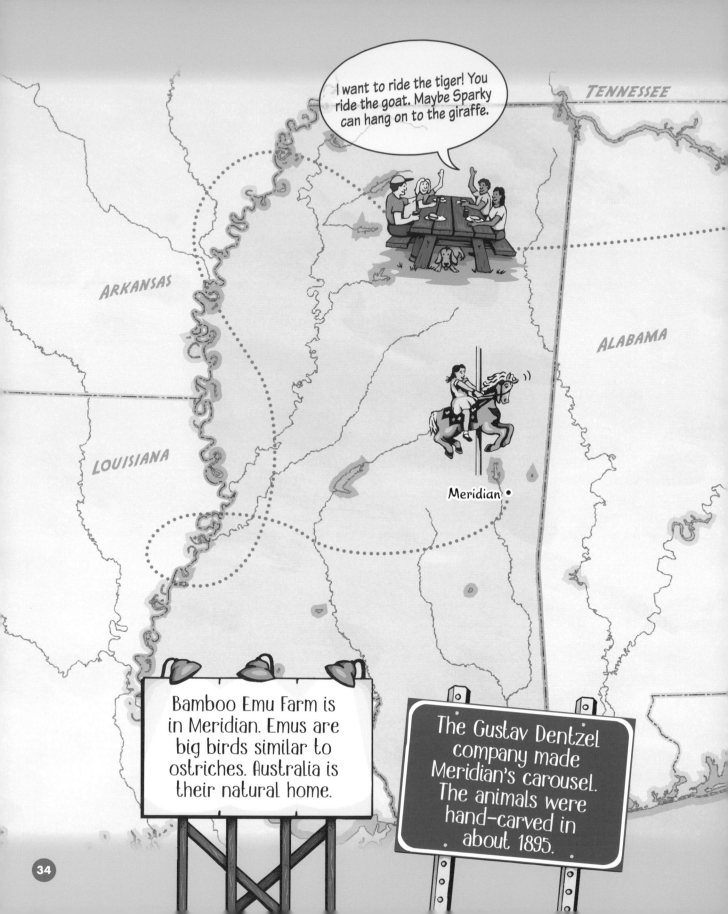

MERIDIAN'S CAROUSEL HORSES

Stroll around Meridian. You're in for some big surprises! Turn a corner, and there's a **carousel** horse. Walk through a park, and there's another horse. You'll find them all over town! There are more than 40 horses in all. Each one is decorated with colorful designs.

Carousels are a big deal in Meridian. The city's Highland Park has a famous carousel. It started turning around in 1909. And it has more than horses. It has tigers, lions, goats, and giraffes, too! Which one would you like to ride?

Take a ride on Meridian's carousel!

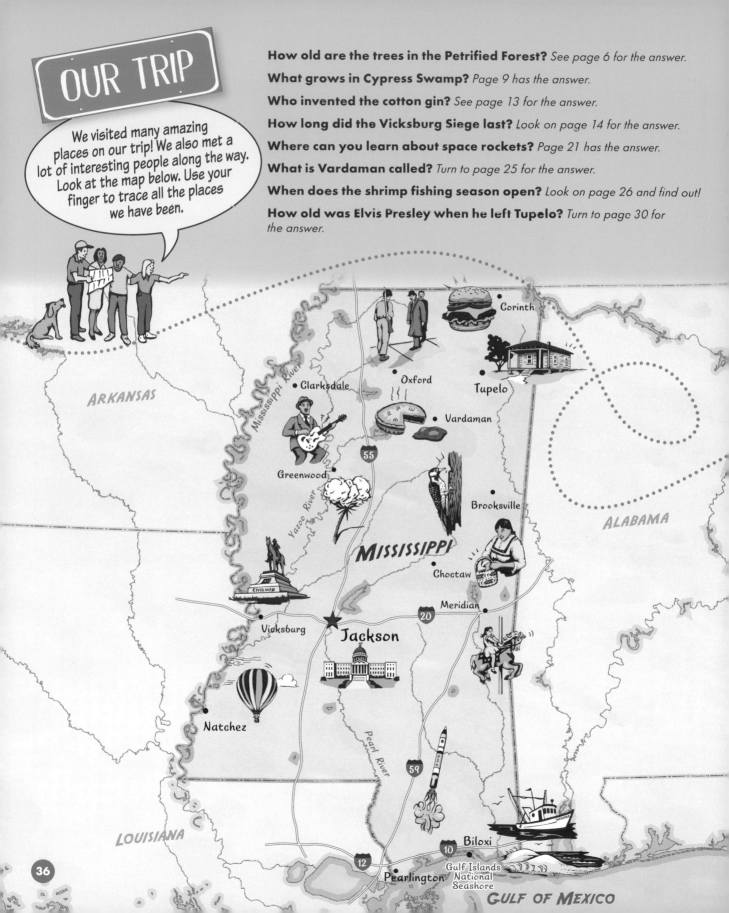

OUR TRIP

We visited many amazing places on our trip! We also met a lot of interesting people along the way. Look at the map below. Use your finger to trace all the places we have been.

How old are the trees in the Petrified Forest? *See page 6 for the answer.*

What grows in Cypress Swamp? *Page 9 has the answer.*

Who invented the cotton gin? *See page 13 for the answer.*

How long did the Vicksburg Siege last? *Look on page 14 for the answer.*

Where can you learn about space rockets? *Page 21 has the answer.*

What is Vardaman called? *Turn to page 25 for the answer.*

When does the shrimp fishing season open? *Look on page 26 and find out!*

How old was Elvis Presley when he left Tupelo? *Turn to page 30 for the answer.*

ARKANSAS

Corinth

Oxford

Tupelo

Clarksdale

Vardaman

MISSISSIPPI

Greenwood

Brooksville

ALABAMA

Choctaw

Meridian

Jackson

Vicksburg

Natchez

Biloxi

Pearlington

Gulf Islands National Seashore

LOUISIANA

GULF OF MEXICO

STATE SYMBOLS

State beverage: Milk

State bird: Mockingbird

State fish: Largemouth bass (black bass)

State flower: Magnolia

State fossil: Prehistoric whale

State insect: Honeybee

State land mammal: White-tailed deer

State shell: Oyster shell

State stone: Petrified wood

State tree: Magnolia

State waterfowl: Wood duck

State water mammal: Bottle-nosed dolphin

State seal

STATE SONG

"GO, MISSISSIPPI"

Words and music by Houston Davis

States may sing their songs of praise
With waving flags and hip-hoo-rays,
Let cymbals crash and let bells ring
'Cause here's one song I'm proud to sing.

Choruses:
Go, Mississippi, keep rolling along,
Go, Mississippi, you cannot go wrong,
Go, Mississippi, we're singing your song,
M-I-S-S-I-S-S-I-P-P-I.

Go, Mississippi, you're on the right track,
Go, Mississippi, and this is a fact,
Go, Mississippi, you'll never look back,
M-I-S-S-I-S-S-I-P-P-I.

Go, Mississippi, straight down the line,
Go, Mississippi, ev'rything's fine,
Go, Mississippi, it's your state and mine,
M-I-S-S-I-S-S-I-P-P-I.

Go, Mississippi, continue to roll,
Go, Mississippi, the top is the goal,
Go, Mississippi, you'll have and you'll hold,
M-I-S-S-I-S-S-I-P-P-I.

Go, Mississippi, get up and go,
Go, Mississippi, let the world know,
That our Mississippi is leading the show,
M-I-S-S-I-S-S-I-P-P-I.

That was a great trip! We have traveled all over Mississippi! There are a few places that we didn't have time for, though. Next time, we plan to visit the Jackson Zoo. You can see exhibits that have red pandas and tigers!

State flag

FAMOUS PEOPLE

Buffett, Jimmy (1946–), musician, songwriter, author, actor, businessman

Diddley, Bo (1928–2008), guitarist, songwriter, singer

Evers, Charles (1922–), civil rights leader

Evers, Medgar (1925–1963), civil rights leader

Faulkner, William (1897–1962), author

Favre, Brett (1969–), football player

Freeman, Morgan (1937–), actor

Henson, Jim (1936–1990), creator of the Muppets

Hill, Faith (1967–), singer

Jones, James Earl (1931–), actor

King, B. B. (1925–2015), blues musician

Payton, Walter (1954–1999), football player

Presley, Elvis (1935–1977), singer

Revels, Hiram Rhoades (1827–1901), first African American elected to U.S. Senate

Spears, Britney (1981–), singer

Taylor, Mildred D. (1943–), children's author

Waters, Muddy (1915–1983), blues musician

Wells-Barnett, Ida B. (1862–1931), journalist, civil rights leader

Welty, Eudora (1909–2001), author

Williams, Tennessee (1911–1983), playwright

Winfrey, Oprah (1954–), talk show host, producer, media mogul

Wynette, Tammy (1942–1998), singer

WORDS TO KNOW

carousel (KAIR-uh-sell) a merry-go-round

civil rights (SIV-il RITES) the rights of a nation's citizens, such as voting and education rights

fawns (FAWNZ) baby deer

fry bread (FRYE-BRED) a deep-fried bread made by Native Americans

hominy (HA-muh-nee) corn kernels that are soaked so they swell up

immigrants (IM-uh-gruhntz) people who move to a new country from their home country

industry (IN-duhs-tree) type of businesses

legends (LEJ-uhndz) stories created to explain mysteries

mansions (MAN-shuhnz) large, elegant homes

plantation (plan-TAY-shuhn) a large farm that raises mainly one crop

riots (RYE-uhts) public disorder by large crowds

sharecroppers (SHAIR-krop-urz) people who rent farmland and pay their rent with crops

wreath (REETH) leaves or flowers woven into a circle

TO LEARN MORE

IN THE LIBRARY

Adoff, Arnold. *Roots and Blues: A Celebration*. New York, NY: Clarion Books, 2011.

Foran, Jill. *Mississippi: The Magnolia State*. New York, NY: AV2 by Weigl, 2016.

Graham Gaines, Ann. *Mississippi*. New York, NY: Cavendish Square, 2014.

Shofner, Shawndra. *Mississippi*. Mankato, MN: Creative Education, 2009.

ON THE WEB

Visit our Web site for links about Mississippi:
childsworld.com/links

Note to Parents, Teachers, and Librarians: We routinely verify our Web links to make sure they are safe and active sites. So encourage your readers to check them out!

PLACES TO VISIT OR CONTACT

The Old Capitol Museum
mdah.ms.gov
100 South State Street
Jackson, MS 39201
601/576-6920
For more information about the history of Mississippi

Visit Mississippi
visitmississippi.org
501 North West Street, Suite 500
Jackson, MS 39201
601/359-3297
For more information about traveling in Mississippi

Mississippi covers 48,432 square miles (125,438 sq km). It's the 32st-largest state in size.

INDEX

Bye, Magnolia State. We had a great time. We'll come back soon!